Published by Creative Education
P.O. Box 227, Mankato, Minnesota 56002
Creative Education is an imprint of
The Creative Company
www.thecreativecompany.us

Design and production by The Design Lab
Art direction by Rita Marshall
Printed by Corporate Graphics
in the United States of America

Photographs by Alamy (Arco Images GmbH, Jan
Csernoch), Getty Images (Shaen Adey, Annie Griffiths
Belt, James Hager, Jeffrey L. Rotman, Art Wolfe),
iStockphoto (Paul Clarke, George Clerk, Jurie Maree,
Thorsten Rust), Minden Pictures (Suzi Eszterhas,
Mike Parry)

Library of Congress Cataloging-in-Publication Data
Bodden, Valerie.
Crocodiles / by Valerie Bodden.
p. cm. — (Amazing animals)
Includes bibliographical references and index.
Summary: A basic exploration of the appearance,
behavior, and habitat of crocodiles, a family of
sharp-toothed reptiles. Also included is a story from
folklore explaining why crocodiles have rough skin.
ISBN 978-1-58341-806-2
1. Crocodiles—Juvenile literature. I. Title. II. Series.
QL666.C925B63 2010
597.98'2—dc22   2009002706

CPSIA: 092110 PO 361

9 8 7 6 5 4 3

AMAZING ANIMALS

CROCODILES

BY VALERIE BODDEN

CREATIVE EDUCATION

Crocodiles spend most
of their lives in water

Crocodiles are big reptiles. They live in water or near water. There are 13 kinds of crocodiles in the world.

reptiles animals that have scales and a body that is
always as warm or as cold as the air around it

Crocodiles are long.
They are wide in the middle and pointy at the ends. Crocodiles are covered with tough, bumpy skin. The skin is tan, brown, or green. Some crocodiles are covered with black patches.

*Crocodiles are protected
by skin that is very hard*

Some crocodiles are very big. They can weigh almost as much as three grown-up men put together. They can be 16 feet (5 m) long. That is longer than a minivan! Other crocodiles are smaller. They are only about five feet (1.5 m) long.

A crocodile's tail makes up about half of its body

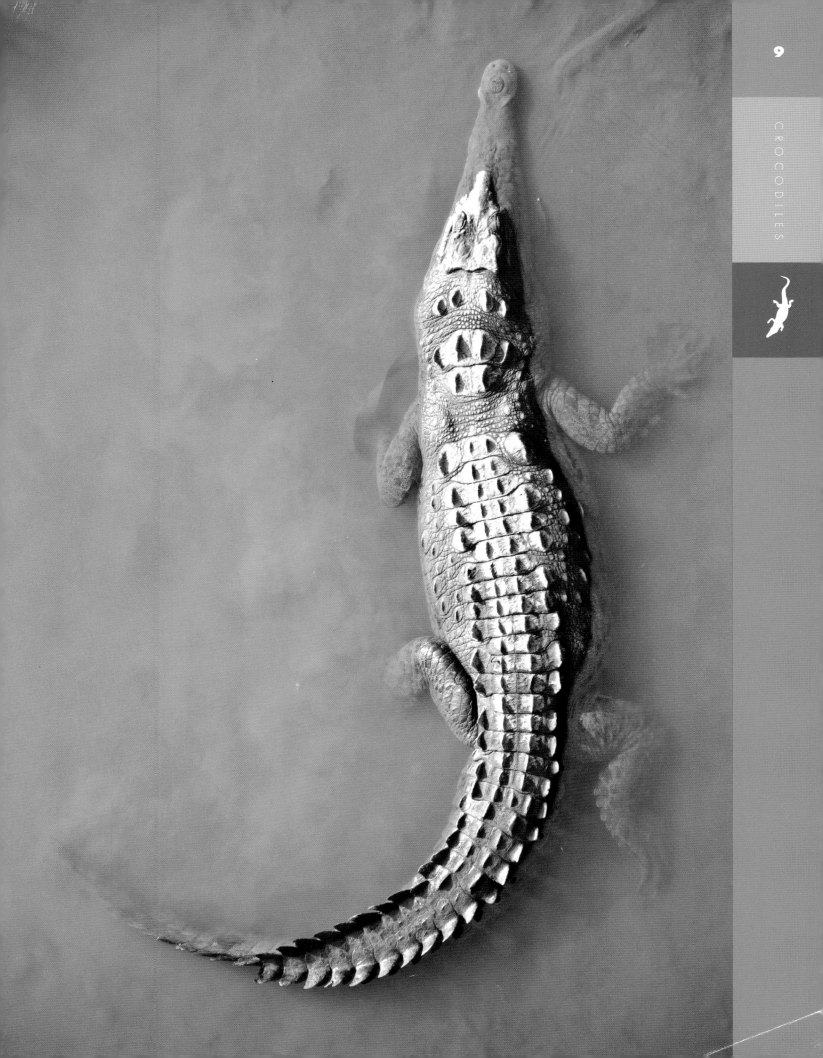

*Crocodiles can jump out
of the water to take a bite*

Crocodiles live in many places around the world. Crocodiles live along the shores of rivers and lakes. They live in **wetlands**, too.

wetlands areas of land where the dirt is always covered with water

Crocodiles eat meat.

They eat small animals such as birds and fish. They eat big animals, too. They can eat animals as big as deer and zebras!

Crocodiles have very strong jaws for biting food

*A mother crocodile can lay
20 to 90 eggs at once*

A mother crocodile lays lots of eggs in a hole. When the eggs **hatch**, baby crocodiles come out. They are smaller than a ruler. Many of the babies are eaten by other animals like eagles. The ones that grow up can live more than 50 years.

hatch break open

Crocodiles spend a lot of their time just lying around. If they are hot, they lie in the shade. If they are cold, they move to a spot in the sun.

Big crocodiles are not afraid of any other animals

Some crocodiles can stay underwater for two hours

Crocodiles

spend time swimming, too. They can swim with just their eyes and **nostrils** above the water. Or they can swim with their whole body under the water. They wave their strong tail back and forth. That pushes them through the water.

nostrils holes in the nose

Today, people around the world go to zoos to see crocodiles. Others go to shows to watch people wrestle crocodiles. Some people watch crocodiles in the wild. It is exciting to see these big reptiles anywhere!

Most big zoos have special areas for crocodiles

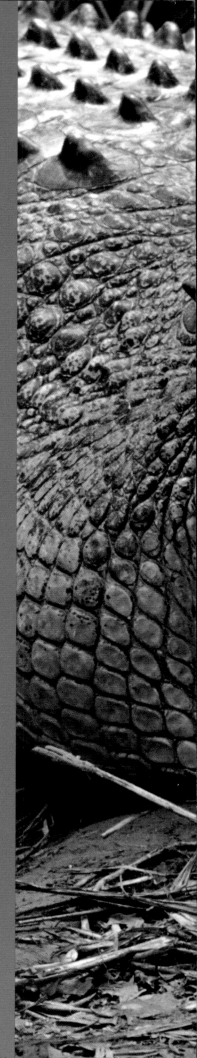

A Crocodile Story

Why do crocodiles have rough skin? People on the **continent** of Africa used to tell a story about this. They said that the crocodile once had smooth skin because he came out only at night. But then the other animals said they liked the crocodile's skin. The crocodile came out during the day to show off his skin. Soon, the sun made the crocodile's skin rough and bumpy, and it stayed that way!

continent one of Earth's seven big pieces of land

Read More

Kaufman, Gabriel. *Saltwater Crocodile: The World's Biggest Reptile*. New York: Bearport, 2007.

Thomas, Isabel. *Alligator vs. Crocodile*. Chicago: Raintree, 2006.

Web Sites

Crocodile Photo Gallery
http://www.flmnh.ufl.edu/natsci/herpetology/crocs/crocodilephotos.htm
This site has lots of pictures of crocodiles.

Enchanted Learning: Alligators and Crocodiles
http://www.enchantedlearning.com/themes/alligator.shtml
This site has alligator and crocodile activities and coloring pages.

Index